THE CIVIL RIGHTS ACT

by Josephine Larsen

EQUAL = RIGHTS

pogo

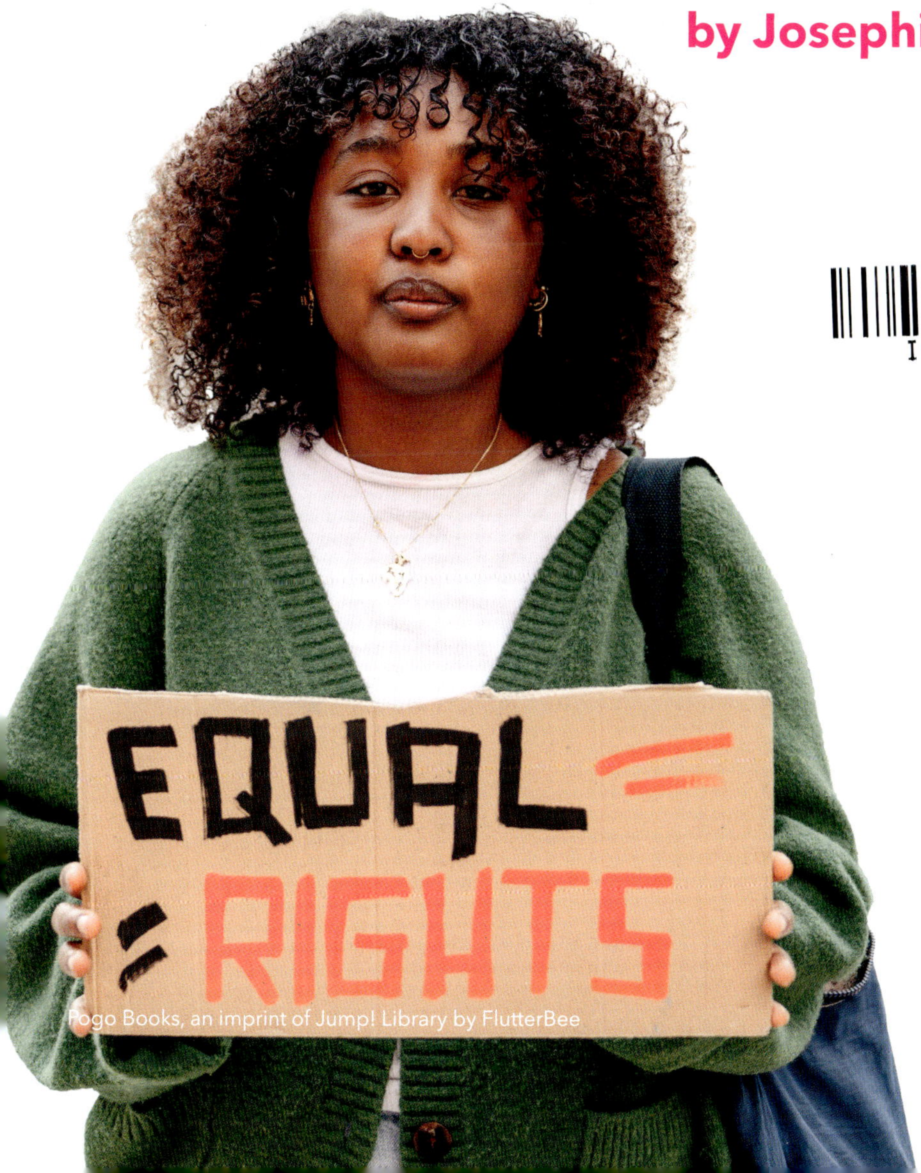

Pogo Books, an imprint of Jump! Library by FlutterBee

Ideas for Parents and Teachers

Pogo Books let children practice reading informational text while introducing them to nonfiction features such as headings, labels, sidebars, maps, and diagrams, as well as a table of contents, glossary, and index.

Carefully leveled text with a strong photo match offers early fluent readers the support they need to succeed.

Before Reading

- "Walk" through the book and point out the various nonfiction features. Ask the student what purpose each feature serves.
- Look at the glossary together. Read and discuss the words.

During Reading

- Have the child read the book independently.
- Invite them to list questions that arise from reading.

After Reading

- Discuss the child's questions. Talk about how they might find answers to those questions.
- Prompt the child to think more. Ask: Why is equality important? What can you do to make sure people are treated equally?

Pogo Books are published by Jump!
3500 American Blvd W, Suite 150
Bloomington, MN 55431
www.jumplibrary.com

Jump! is a division of FlutterBee Education Group.

Library of Congress Cataloging-in-Publication Data

Names: Larsen, Josephine author
Title: The Civil Rights Act / Josephine Larsen.
Description: Bloomington, MN: Jump!, Inc., 2026.
Series: Writing that changed U.S. history
Includes index.
Audience: Ages 7-10
Identifiers: LCCN 2025034503 (print)
LCCN 2025034504 (ebook)
ISBN 9798896623434 hardcover
ISBN 9798896623441 paperback
ISBN 9798896623458 ebook
Subjects: LCSH: United States. Civil Rights Act of 1964–Juvenile literature | Civil rights–United States–History–Juvenile literature | Equality before the law–United States–Juvenile literature | Segregation–Law and legislation–United States–History–20th century–Juvenile literature | Civil rights movements–United States–History–20th century–Juvenile literature
Classification: LCC KF4744.5151964 .L37 2026 (print)
LCC KF4744.5151964 (ebook)
DDC 342.7308/509–dc23/eng/20250729
LC record available at https://lccn.loc.gov/2025034503
LC ebook record available at https://lccn.loc.gov/2025034504

Editor: Alyssa Sorenson
Designer: Emma Almgren-Bersie

Photo Credits: National Archives, cover (document); mato181/Shutterstock, cover (flag); LeoPatrizi iStock, 1; Library of Congress, 3, 6-7, 8-9; Bettmann Getty, 4; AP Images, 5; Marco_Piunti/iStock, 10; AnnaStills/iStock, 11; SeventyFour/Shutterstock, 12-13; Tongpool Piasupun/Shutterstock, 14-15; Manop Boonpeng/Shutterstock, 16-17; Mark Mulligan/Houston Chronicle/Hearst Newspapers/Getty, 18-19; traveler1116/iStock, 20; Marcos Elihu Castillo Ramirez/iStock, 21; Daniel Thornberg/Adobe Stock, 23.

Printed in the United States of America at Corporate Graphics in North Mankato, Minnesota.

TABLE OF CONTENTS

CHAPTER 1

FIGHTING FOR EQUAL RIGHTS

In the 1960s, **discrimination** was a big problem in the United States. People of color were treated unfairly. Many white people would not give them jobs. If they did, they did not pay them as much as white people.

We Don't Buy Where We Can't Work

Some states made it hard for people of color to vote. Why? White people did not want people of color to have a say in government. They made them take tests. They made them pay money to vote.

Some states were **segregated**. Laws separated Black and white people. They could not go to the same schools, restaurants, and more. They could not drink from the same water coolers. Spaces for Black people were not as nice.

TAKE A LOOK!

Which states were segregated in the 1950s? Take a look.

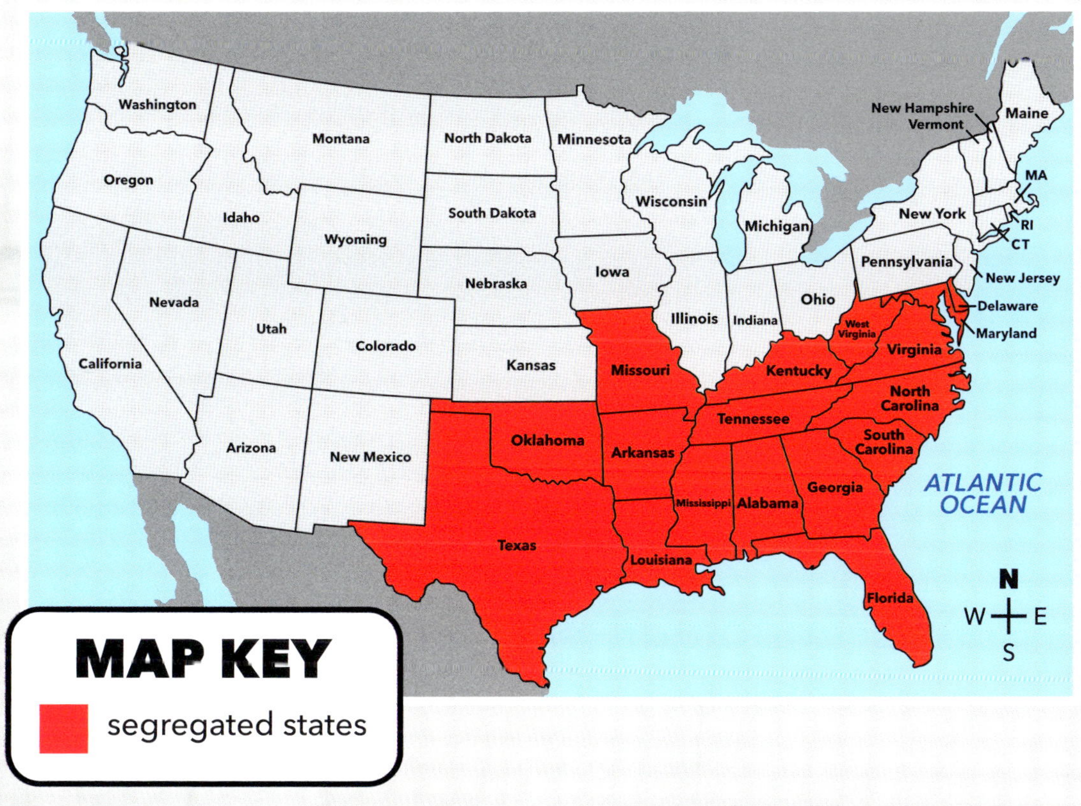

MAP KEY

segregated states

People wanted change. They led the **Civil Rights** Movement. They spoke out. They **protested**. They were peaceful. They **boycotted** businesses that did not welcome Black people. More people saw how unfair things were for people of color.

In 1964, **Congress** made the Civil Rights Act. Why? It wanted to stop discrimination.

WHAT DO YOU THINK?

People in the Civil Rights Movement made their voices heard. They spoke out. They made signs. Would you make your voice heard? How?

WE MARCH FOR INTEGRATED SCHOOLS NOW!
WE DEMAND DECENT HOUSING NOW!
WE DEMAND AN END TO BIAS NOW!
WE DEMAND AN END TO POLICE BRUTALITY NOW!
UAW SAYS JOBS and FREEDOM FOR Every American
FREEDOM IN '63

CHAPTER 2

ACTS FOR EQUALITY

The Civil Rights Act is about **equality**. It says many kinds of discrimination are **illegal**.

The Act has 11 parts. They are called titles. Title One is about voting rights. It says states cannot make people pass tests to vote. It says people of all **races** can vote.

Hello Monday

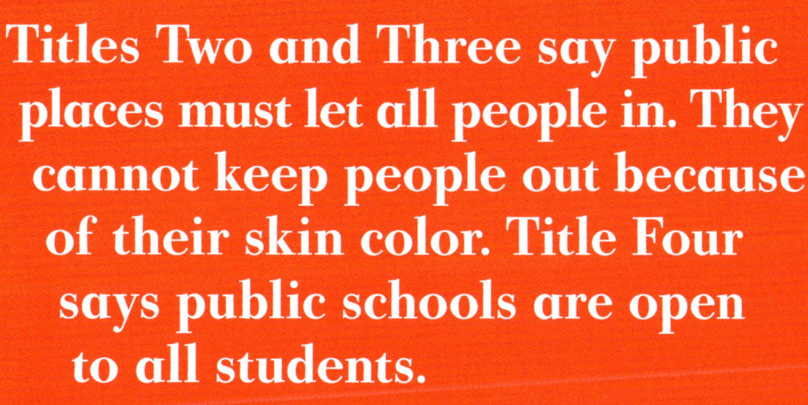

Titles Two and Three say public places must let all people in. They cannot keep people out because of their skin color. Title Four says public schools are open to all students.

WHAT DO YOU THINK?

How would you feel if you could not go into a building because of the way you looked?

The Commission on Civil Rights is a group. It was made in 1957. It stands up for people who are not treated equally. It can make reports to the U.S. president and Congress. Title Five gave it more power and money.

Title Six says government programs must treat everyone equally. This includes health care.

DOCTOR

Title Seven is about jobs. It says employers must be fair. They cannot hire, fire, or **promote** people based on race, skin color, gender, or religion.

DID YOU KNOW?

In 2020, the **U.S. Supreme Court** said companies cannot fire people for being gay, lesbian, or **transgender**. Why? Title Seven protects them.

The last sections make sure people follow civil rights laws. Title Eight says the United States must collect voting **data** by race. Why? It helps the government see who votes. It makes sure everyone has a chance to.

Title Nine says the United States can make sure courts treat laws fairly. Title Ten started the Community Relations Service. This helps **communities** that face discrimination. Title Eleven says people who break civil rights laws can have a fair **trial**.

Judge George Powell
351st District Criminal Court

CHAPTER 3

STILL FIGHTING

Discrimination is illegal in the United States. But it is still a problem. People still fight for equality. If people break the Civil Rights Act, they get in trouble. They can go to court.

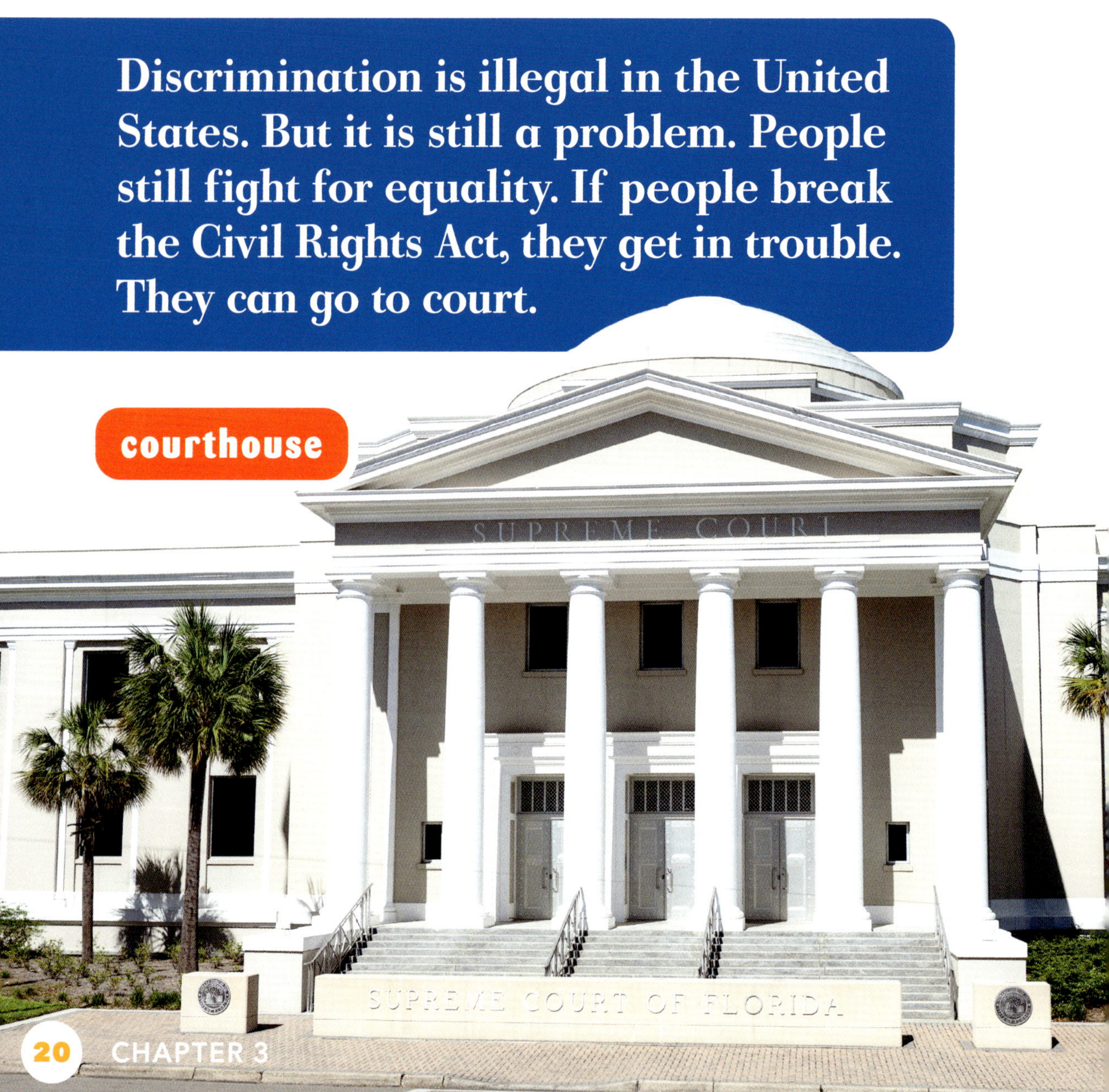

courthouse

The Civil Rights Act showed other groups they can get more rights. Older people, people with disabilities, and pregnant women fought for equality. New laws were passed. These people now have more rights at work and in public places. We must work together for equality. How can you help?

QUICK FACTS & TOOLS

TIMELINE

What are important dates in the history of the Civil Rights Act? Take a look!

MAY 17, 1954
The U.S. Supreme Court says segregation in schools is illegal. White schools are told to let Black students in. It takes years for this to happen.

DECEMBER 1, 1955
A Black woman named Rosa Parks is arrested for not giving her bus seat to a white person. This starts a bus boycott in Montgomery, Alabama.

1957
The Commission on Civil Rights is created.

AUGUST 28, 1963
More than 260,000 people go to Washington, D.C. They demand equal rights. This is called the March on Washington for Jobs and Freedom.

1964
Congress creates the Civil Rights Act. On July 2, President Lyndon B. Johnson signs it into law.

GLOSSARY

boycotted: Refused to buy something or do business with someone as a punishment or protest.

civil rights: Things citizens are guaranteed and able to do.

communities: Groups of people who live in the same place or share something important, like culture, interests, or experiences.

Congress: The part of the U.S. government that makes laws.

data: Information collected so something can be done with it.

discrimination: Prejudice or unfair behavior toward people based on differences in things such as age, race, or gender.

equality: The right for everyone to be treated the same.

illegal: Against the law.

promote: To give someone a higher job with more money.

protested: Demonstrated against something.

races: Groups people are divided into based on their appearance.

segregated: Separated or kept apart from the main group.

transgender: Having a different gender identity than what you were given at birth.

trial: The examination of evidence in a court of law to decide if someone is guilty or innocent.

U.S. Supreme Court: The highest U.S. court that upholds the U.S. Constitution and laws.

INDEX

TO LEARN MORE

Finding more information is as easy as 1, 2, 3.

1. Go to www.factsurfer.com
2. Enter "Civil Rights Act" into the search box.
3. Choose your book to see a list of websites.